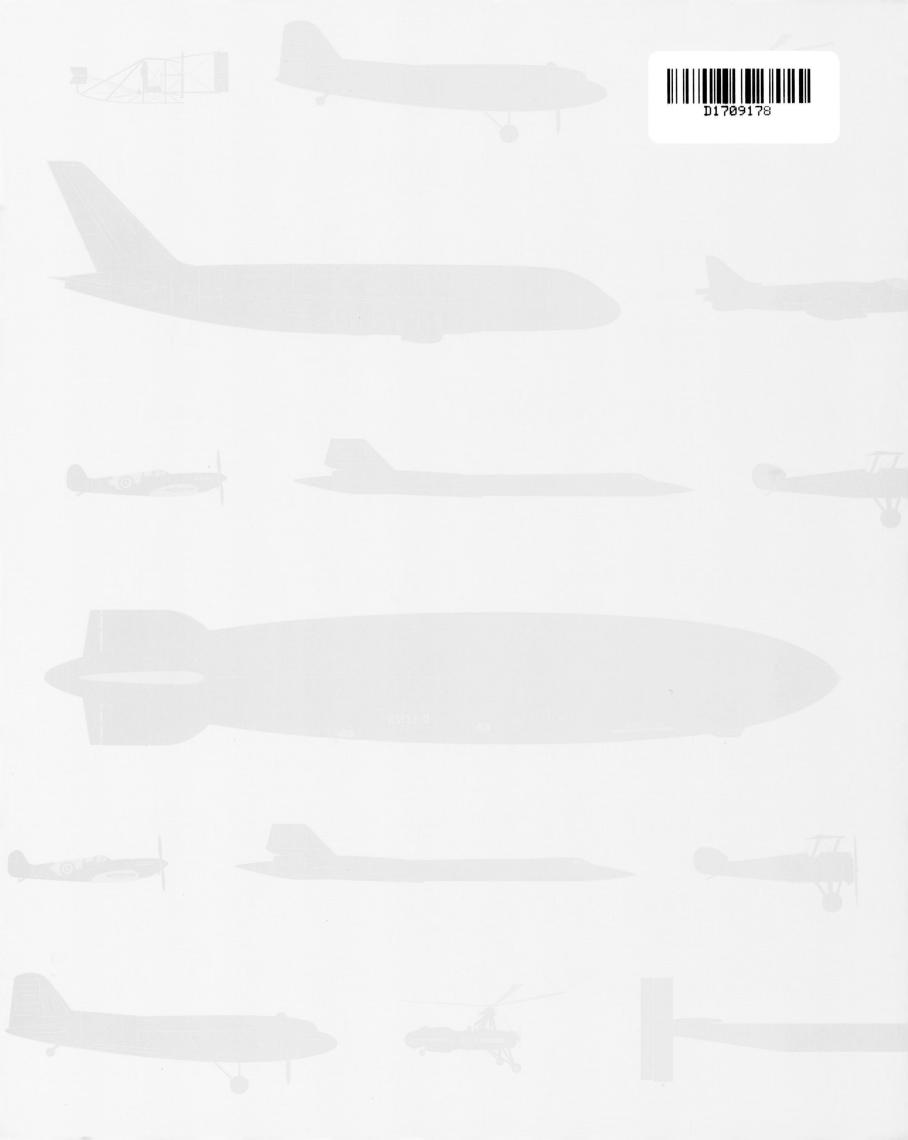

The Story of Flight

Written by **JAKOB WHITFIELD**

Illustrated by **US NOW**

wren
&rook

1853
1890
1903
1910
1914
1919
1947
197

First published in Great Britain in 2019 by Wren & Rook

Text and design copyright © Hodder and Stoughton Limited, 2019
Illustration copyright © Brian Roberts, 2019

ISBN: 978 1 5263 6022 9
E-book ISBN: 978 1 5263 6079 3
10 9 8 7 6 5 4 3 2

Wren & Rook
An imprint of
Hachette Children's Group
Part of Hodder & Stoughton
Carmelite House
50 Victoria Embankment
London EC4Y 0DZ

An Hachette UK Company
www.hachette.co.uk
www.hachettechildrens.co.uk

Publishing Director: Debbie Foy
Senior Editor: Liza Miller
Art Director: Laura Hambleton
Designer: Brian Roberts

Printed in China

Picture acknowledgements: The publisher would like to thank the following for
permission to reproduce their pictures: QVectors / Shutterstock.com 24–25

Contents

Dreams of Flight

THROUGHOUT HISTORY, HUMANS HAVE LOOKED UP AT BIRDS AND DREAMED OF FLIGHT.

From ancient myth and legend to modern superhero movies, to soar on the winds and gaze down at the Earth is the power of gods, monsters and caped crusaders. However, storytellers have always known that achieving flight is a risky undertaking.

In ancient Greek mythology, the inventor Daedalus built a Labyrinth, an elaborate maze, for cruel King Minos of Crete. But the king imprisoned Daedalus and his son Icarus after they enraged him.

To escape, Daedalus built bird-like wings made of wood, feathers and wax. He warned his son not to fly too high (the Sun would soften the wax) or too low (the sea's spray would soak the feathers).

Once airborne, however, Icarus was intoxicated by the sensation of flight. Ignoring his father's warnings, he soared higher and higher, ever closer to the Sun. The wax melted and Icarus plunged to the blue sea far below.

Though human flight remained the stuff of dreams for thousands of years, Icarus's desire inspired many attempts to fly with the birds.

1853

Birdmen

EARLY FLYERS TRIED TO COPY THE FLAPPING MOTIONS OF BIRDS, STRAPPING WINGS OR SAILS TO THEIR ARMS AND LEGS BEFORE JUMPING FROM HIGH PLACES.

Unfortunately, humans don't have the same powerful muscles that birds do; without the power to keep themselves up or the ability to properly steer their path, most of these 'birdmen' suffered serious injury or death.

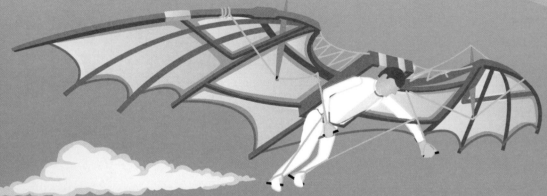

During the Renaissance, famous artist and inventor Leonardo da Vinci was fascinated by bird flight. He designed an **ORNITHOPTER** that used the flyer's arms and legs to flap the machine's wings.

However, it took until the nineteenth century for experimenters to copy the flight of birds as they glided rather than flapped. In 1853, British landowner Sir George Cayley built a glider that his coachman flew across a valley; after landing, the servant stepped out and said, 'I wish to give notice. I was hired to drive, and not to fly!'

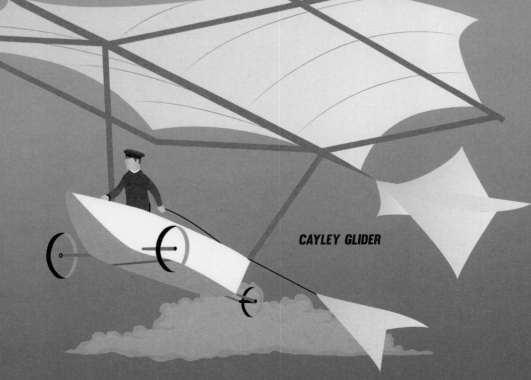

CAYLEY GLIDER

MONTGOLFIER BALLOON

Ballooning

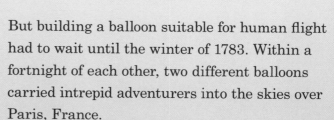

THE PRINCIPLE OF THE HOT-AIR BALLOON IS AN ANCIENT ONE; BAMBOO SKY LANTERNS WERE USED IN CHINA BEFORE THE FIRST CENTURY CE.

But building a balloon suitable for human flight had to wait until the winter of 1783. Within a fortnight of each other, two different balloons carried intrepid adventurers into the skies over Paris, France.

Joseph and Étienne Montgolfier built the first. They made their hot air balloon from richly decorated paper-backed linen. More than 20 metres tall, it carried courtiers François Laurent, Marquis d'Arlandes and Jean-François Pilâtre de Rozier for 9 kilometres.

CHARLES BALLOON

Jacques Charles's hydrogen balloon soon followed. As a physicist, Charles knew that hydrogen gas was about 16 times lighter than air, so a balloon filled with hydrogen could be smaller than an air balloon while still having the same lifting power. On its first voyage, Charles and a companion flew more than 40 km.

In the years that followed, balloons were used for daring feats, such as the first Channel crossing in 1785. And in wartime, they spotted enemy positions from above. But balloons were an impractical mode of travel because they could not be steered.

Floating on the Breeze

WHEN LIGHTWEIGHT ENGINES WERE DEVELOPED IN THE 1800S, INGENIOUS BALLOON INVENTORS FITTED THEM TO THE BASKETS OF THEIR DESIGNS SO PILOTS COULD CHANGE DIRECTION. THE BALLOONS OF THESE 'DIRIGIBLES' — MEANING 'STEERABLE CRAFT' — ALSO BECAME LONGER, TO BETTER SLIP THROUGH THE AIR.

Before long, balloons large enough to carry a useful load of cargo and passengers were being developed. However, these vast balloons were fragile and unwieldy. A sturdy frame to safely enclose multiple balloons — also known as gasbags — was a handy solution.

SANTOS-DUMONT NO. 6

The most famous of these rigid airships were those built by visionary **COUNT FERDINAND VON ZEPPELIN**, who first started building them in the 1890s. Many of his early designs crashed, so the German government stopped supporting him.

1890

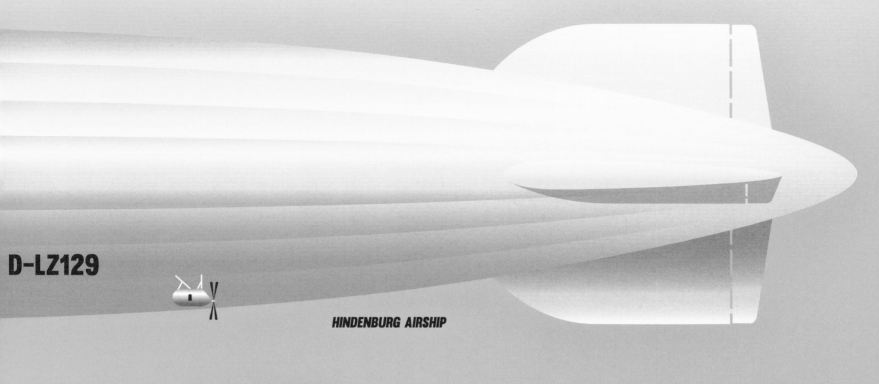

D-LZ129

HINDENBURG AIRSHIP

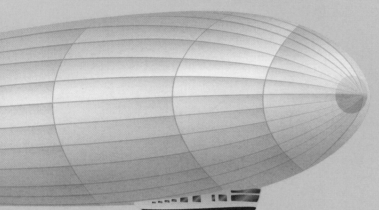

GRAF ZEPPELIN

But Count Zeppelin's success had become a matter of national pride, and a fundraising appeal to the public allowed him to complete his airships. In 1910, he was finally able to launch the world's first passenger airline.

In the 1920s and 1930s, the giant **ZEPPELINS** ran revolutionary international passenger services across the Atlantic. They carried around 60 passengers in luxury, just like an ocean liner, but were twice as fast: the journey was completed in just two or three days.

However, they still relied on highly flammable hydrogen gas for lift. In 1937, the **ZEPPELIN HINDENBURG** caught fire and exploded on landing. Unfortunately 36 people died, and film footage and photos of the burning airship were shown around the world.

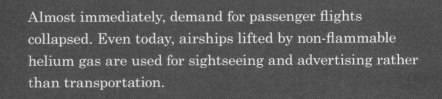

Almost immediately, demand for passenger flights collapsed. Even today, airships lifted by non-flammable helium gas are used for sightseeing and advertising rather than transportation.

1903

WRIGHT FLYER

Inventing the Aeroplane

AFTER GEORGE CAYLEY'S SERVANT TOOK TO THE SKY, THERE WERE FEW SERIOUS ATTEMPTS AT WINGED FLIGHT FOR NEARLY 50 YEARS. BUT IN 1903, TWO INVENTORS FROM THE UNITED STATES OF AMERICA TOOK UP THE CHALLENGE.

Wilbur Wright's coat flapped in the cold wind coming off the Atlantic. Next to him, his brother Orville lay on the steering cradle of their machine, a flimsy-looking contraption made of wood and fabric. The **FLYER'S** engine roared, and Wilbur started to run alongside as the machine accelerated down its launch track.

It was their third year at Kitty Hawk in North Carolina, USA. Orville and Wilbur had gone there to test their flying machines every year since 1900. Before they started building their designs, they wrote to anyone working in the field to find out what was already known.

They concluded that, along with wings to keep it in the air and an engine to push it along, an aeroplane needed a control system to steer it; the pilot would have to keep it in balance as it flew.

Wilbur carried on running, then stopped and turned; against the headwind, the **FLYER** moved slowly, but it was up in the air – it flew! That night, he sent a telegram home:

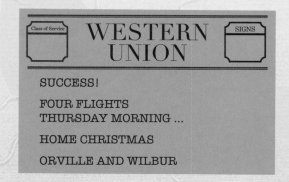

Class of Service	WESTERN UNION	SIGNS

SUCCESS!

FOUR FLIGHTS THURSDAY MORNING ...

HOME CHRISTMAS

ORVILLE AND WILBUR

News of the Wrights' success spread around the world, and other inventors began to try and build their own flying machines. The fact that most of them were far less accomplished than the Wrights' didn't matter – the dream of powered flight was now a reality!

Flying as Fashion

LIKE BICYCLES AND MOTOR CARS BEFORE THEM, AEROPLANES WERE INITIALLY EMBRACED BY RICH ENTHUSIASTS WHO TREATED FLYING AS A SPORT.

Air displays where pilots set speed and distance records became hugely popular spectator events. Sir Charles Rolls was typical: a racing cyclist while at university, he co-founded the **ROLLS-ROYCE** company to make cars, and soon took up ballooning and flying. He was killed in a tragic accident in 1910 when his **WRIGHT FLYER** crashed at a flying exhibition in Bournemouth, UK.

Though most early sport pilots and aircraft manufacturers were wealthy men, enthusiasts from outside this exclusive group could sometimes find ways to fund their dreams. Flying schools sprang up alongside aircraft builders, and poorer pilots could often make money through exhibition and stunt flying.

BLÉRIOT XI

1910

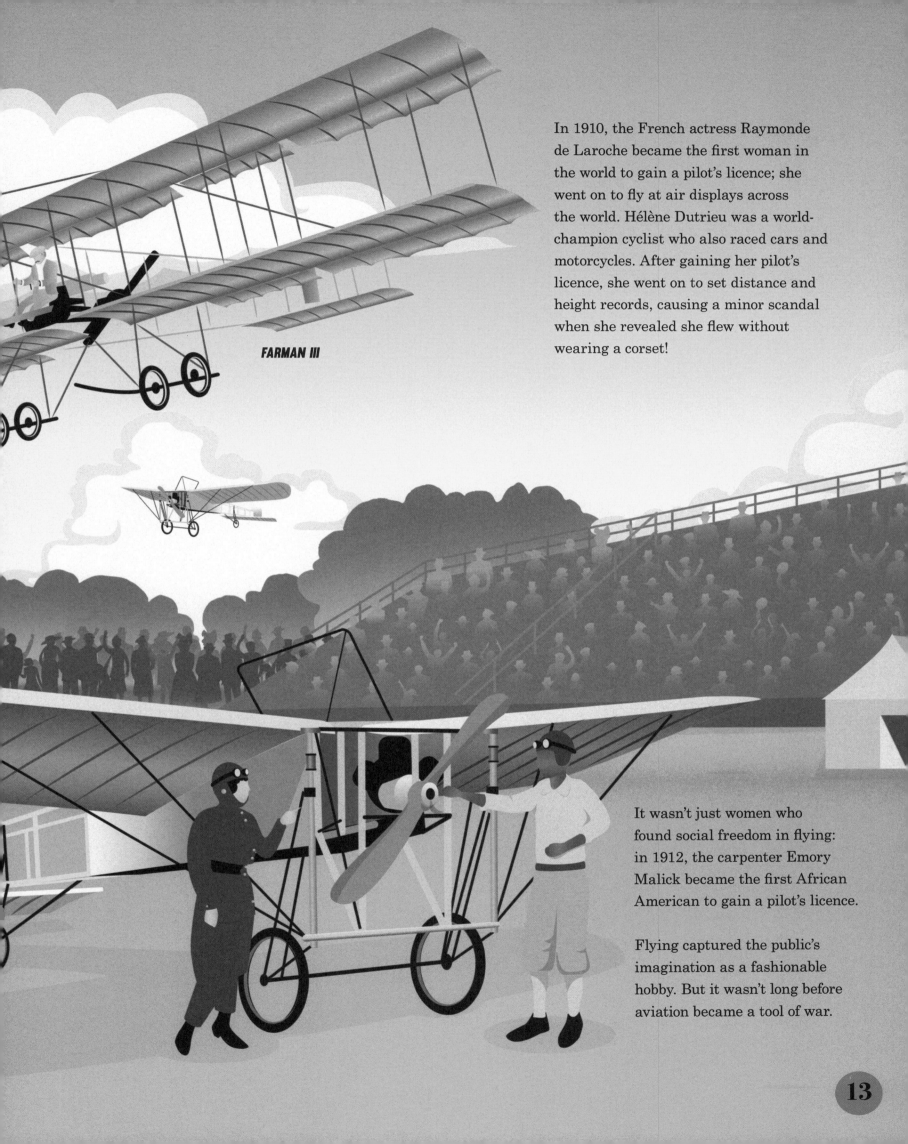

In 1910, the French actress Raymonde de Laroche became the first woman in the world to gain a pilot's licence; she went on to fly at air displays across the world. Hélène Dutrieu was a world-champion cyclist who also raced cars and motorcycles. After gaining her pilot's licence, she went on to set distance and height records, causing a minor scandal when she revealed she flew without wearing a corset!

FARMAN III

It wasn't just women who found social freedom in flying: in 1912, the carpenter Emory Malick became the first African American to gain a pilot's licence.

Flying captured the public's imagination as a fashionable hobby. But it wasn't long before aviation became a tool of war.

13

RFC BE.2C

The First World War

THE AEROPLANE'S POTENTIAL AS A WEAPON OF WAR HAD BEEN RECOGNISED FROM THE MOMENT IT WAS INVENTED; INDEED, THE WRIGHT BROTHERS HAD TRIED TO SELL THEIR DESIGNS TO ARMIES OF DIFFERENT NATIONS.

By the start of the First World War in 1914, many weapon manufacturers were starting to build aircraft. At first, the main use for aeroplanes was to scout out the battlefield.

At the Battle of the Marne, aircraft spotted the German army, allowing French and British soldiers to halt its advance. Before long, planes were carrying weapons to attack targets, or even fight other aircraft.

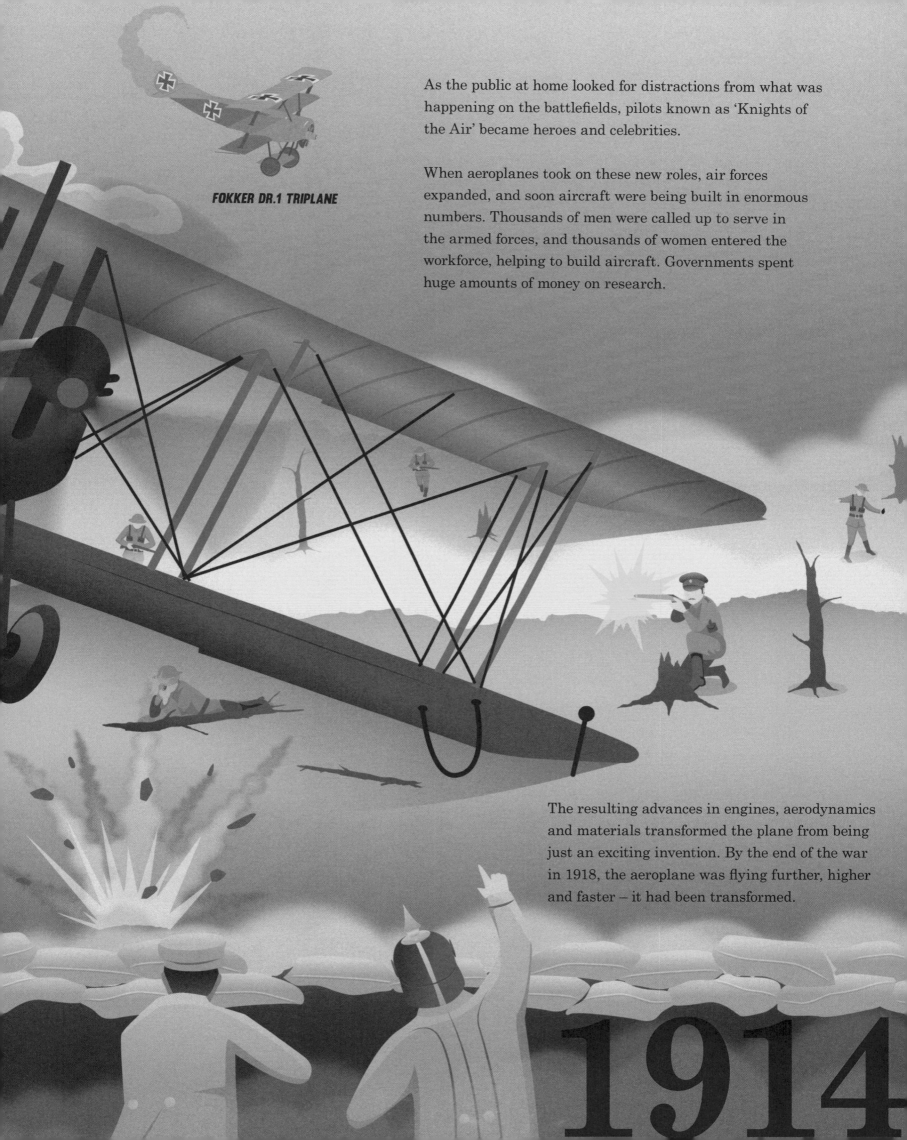

As the public at home looked for distractions from what was happening on the battlefields, pilots known as 'Knights of the Air' became heroes and celebrities.

When aeroplanes took on these new roles, air forces expanded, and soon aircraft were being built in enormous numbers. Thousands of men were called up to serve in the armed forces, and thousands of women entered the workforce, helping to build aircraft. Governments spent huge amounts of money on research.

FOKKER DR.1 TRIPLANE

The resulting advances in engines, aerodynamics and materials transformed the plane from being just an exciting invention. By the end of the war in 1918, the aeroplane was flying further, higher and faster – it had been transformed.

1914

Sleekness and Strength

BOEING 247

DOUGLAS DC-3

DURING THE FIRST WORLD WAR, AIRCRAFT HAD BECOME BIGGER AND HEAVIER OUT OF NECESSITY, BUT THE SCIENCE BEHIND FLIGHT HAD NOT NECESSARILY KEPT UP.

When the fighting finished in 1918, research institutions could finally devote time to better understanding flight. Scientists used a mix of *things* – like wind tunnels, in which aeroplanes could be tested – and *ideas* – new ways of using maths to calculate air flows – to understand how to make aeroplanes more efficient. This new study of aerodynamics meant that aircraft shapes became smooth to slip through the air.

Aeroplanes changed in other ways as well. Early aircraft used frames of wood or steel; these were covered in fabric to give a smooth surface. New constructions had 'stressed-skin' structures instead, meaning the outer surfaces of wings and fuselages were made from panels of wood or metal. Unlike fabric, these could take some of the load from the internal frames, making for lighter and stronger overall structures.

Designers began to use newly discovered metals such as aluminium alloys for building aeroplanes; metals were seen as the materials of the future.

Stronger structures meant designers could build even sleeker aeroplanes; 'biplanes' with their wings stacked above one another began to give way to single-winged planes. The stage was set for thrilling flights of record-breaking adventure and discovery.

SOPWITH CAMEL

17

Spectacle and Adventure

RECORD BREAKERS

Once planes improved, long-distance records sat within reach. The first crossing of the Atlantic was achieved in 1919, and the first Pacific crossing followed in 1928.

DE HAVILLAND GIPSY MOTH

For some distance flights, pilots used aircraft designed to break records, but others used standard planes: in 1930, Amy Johnson became the first woman to fly from Britain to Australia, using a second-hand **DE HAVILLAND GIPSY MOTH**, a light biplane used mostly by flying clubs.

However, after the First World War, governments began to see record attempts as ways to show off national power. From 1918, air, speed and height world records were mainly achieved by military aircraft and pilots.

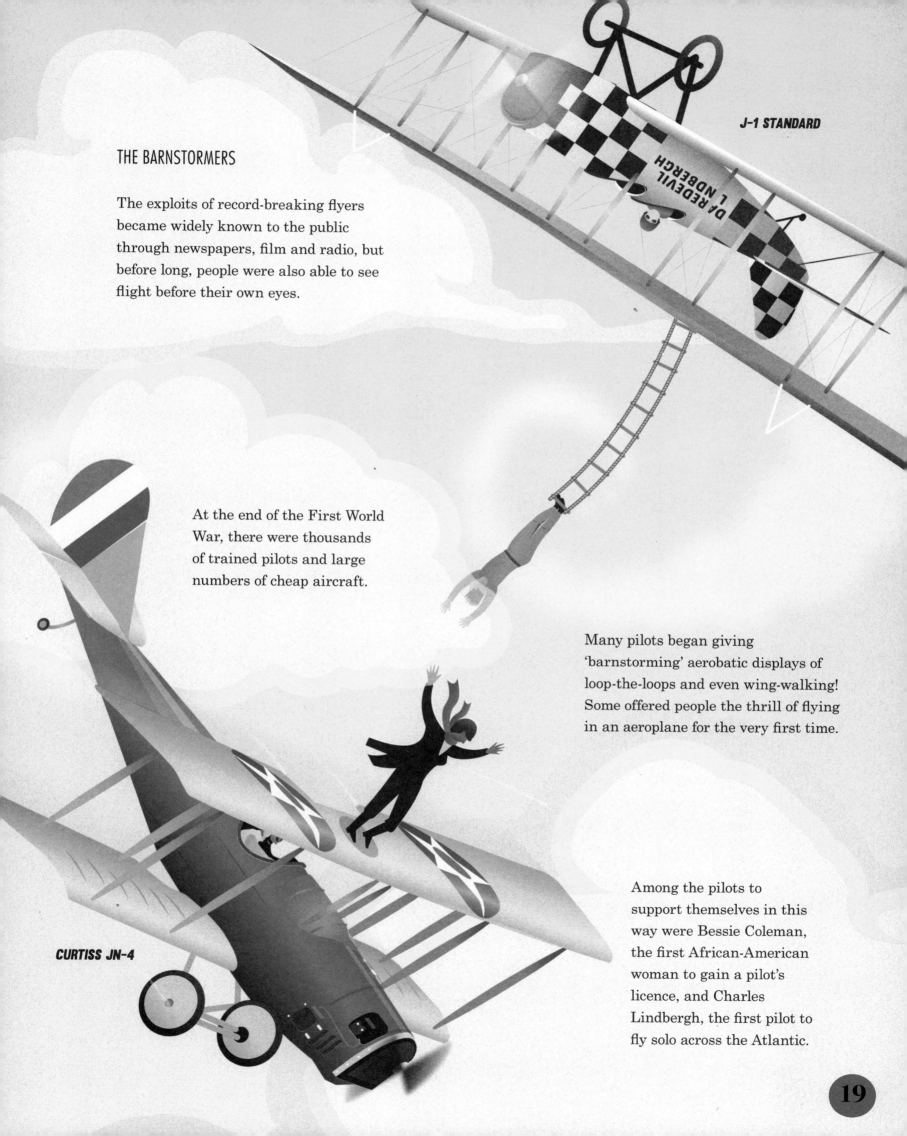

J-1 STANDARD

THE BARNSTORMERS

The exploits of record-breaking flyers became widely known to the public through newspapers, film and radio, but before long, people were also able to see flight before their own eyes.

At the end of the First World War, there were thousands of trained pilots and large numbers of cheap aircraft.

Many pilots began giving 'barnstorming' aerobatic displays of loop-the-loops and even wing-walking! Some offered people the thrill of flying in an aeroplane for the very first time.

CURTISS JN-4

Among the pilots to support themselves in this way were Bessie Coleman, the first African-American woman to gain a pilot's licence, and Charles Lindbergh, the first pilot to fly solo across the Atlantic.

19

JUNKERS JU. 88

MESSERSCHMITT BF 109

The Second World War

FROM 1939–45, THE WORLD DESCENDED INTO WAR AGAIN.

But this time, aircraft weren't just limited to the
battlefield – they were a source of danger to civilians
living in towns and cities too. The changes didn't stop
there; just like in the First World War, governments
spent huge amounts on research, leading to new
technologies such as jet engines and radar.

Radar relied on the fact that aircraft reflected radio
waves, and so could be detected both at long ranges
and in bad weather. The British Royal Air Force (RAF)
was the first armed force to build a system to use this
information. In the Battle of Britain in 1940, radar
helped the RAF's *SPITFIRES* and *HURRICANES* defeat
the bombers of the German Luftwaffe.

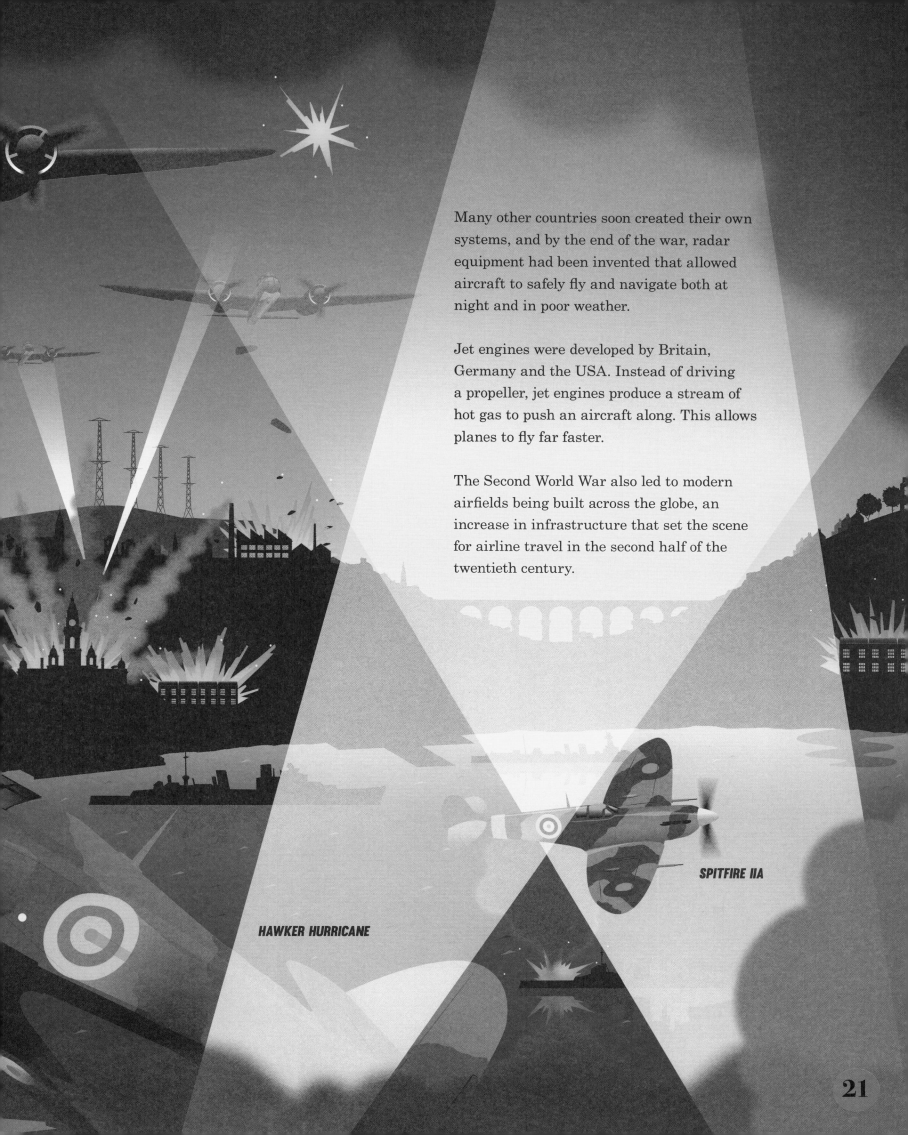

Many other countries soon created their own systems, and by the end of the war, radar equipment had been invented that allowed aircraft to safely fly and navigate both at night and in poor weather.

Jet engines were developed by Britain, Germany and the USA. Instead of driving a propeller, jet engines produce a stream of hot gas to push an aircraft along. This allows planes to fly far faster.

The Second World War also led to modern airfields being built across the globe, an increase in infrastructure that set the scene for airline travel in the second half of the twentieth century.

HAWKER HURRICANE

SPITFIRE IIA

1947

The Need for Speed

DURING THE SECOND WORLD WAR, SOME FIGHTER AIRCRAFT FLYING AT VERY HIGH SPEEDS BEGAN TO GO INTO DANGEROUS UNEXPECTED DIVES.

As the airflow over their wings approached the speed of sound (around 1,000 km per hour), shockwaves started to form, making the aircraft uncontrollable.

When the war ended, researchers set out to beat the 'sound barrier' by shaping the aircraft and its wings to delay or weaken the shockwaves.

In October 1947, American test pilot Chuck Yeager flew a bright orange rocket-powered research plane, the **BELL X-1**, at 1,100 kph – and through the sound barrier.

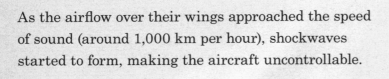

BELL X-1

Before long, rocket- and jet-powered supersonic aeroplanes were reaching dizzying speeds and heights; within a decade of Yeager's flight, aircraft were flying at over twice the speed of sound.

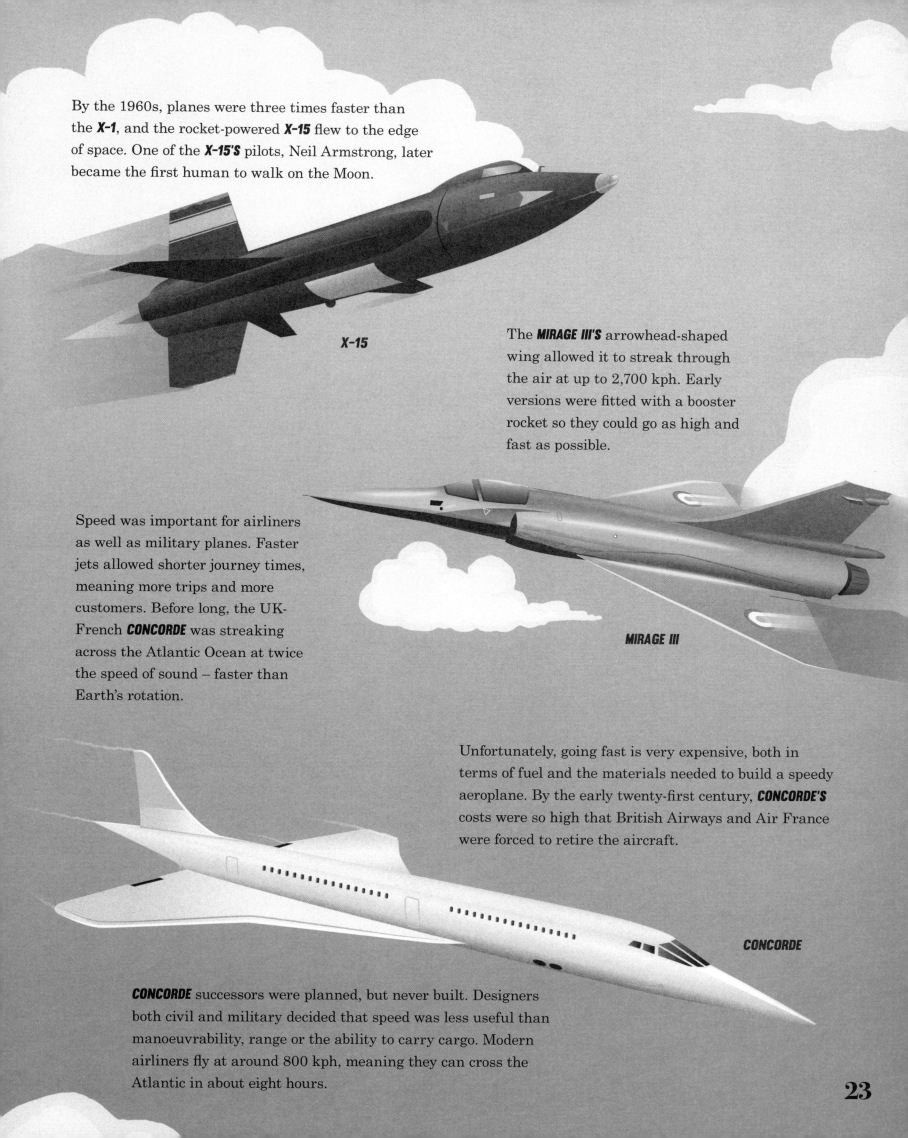

By the 1960s, planes were three times faster than the **X-1**, and the rocket-powered **X-15** flew to the edge of space. One of the **X-15'S** pilots, Neil Armstrong, later became the first human to walk on the Moon.

X-15

The **MIRAGE III'S** arrowhead-shaped wing allowed it to streak through the air at up to 2,700 kph. Early versions were fitted with a booster rocket so they could go as high and fast as possible.

Speed was important for airliners as well as military planes. Faster jets allowed shorter journey times, meaning more trips and more customers. Before long, the UK-French **CONCORDE** was streaking across the Atlantic Ocean at twice the speed of sound – faster than Earth's rotation.

MIRAGE III

Unfortunately, going fast is very expensive, both in terms of fuel and the materials needed to build a speedy aeroplane. By the early twenty-first century, **CONCORDE'S** costs were so high that British Airways and Air France were forced to retire the aircraft.

CONCORDE

CONCORDE successors were planned, but never built. Designers both civil and military decided that speed was less useful than manoeuvrability, range or the ability to carry cargo. Modern airliners fly at around 800 kph, meaning they can cross the Atlantic in about eight hours.

Global Air Travel

BEFORE THE SECOND WORLD WAR, AIR TRAVEL HAD BEEN A LUXURY
FORM OF TRANSPORT.

The experience was often modelled on other glamorous forms of
transport such as ocean liners, with stewards serving meals
on fine china and sleeper cabins for the passengers.

Long-distance flights could cost as much as an average worker's
wages for a whole year. An airline journey from the UK to
Australia took 30 or so stops over 12 days, but this was still
much faster than the journey by boat, which took over a month.

When the war ended, flying was still mainly for the rich, but
passenger numbers began to climb. The huge number of airbases
built during the Second World War meant there were more
destinations available, and modern airliners were also cheaper
to operate, bringing ticket prices down.

At first, all passengers in a plane had to fly in the same class,
but in the 1950s, airlines introduced 'tourist' fares offering a
less luxurious service for a cheaper ticket on the same flight.

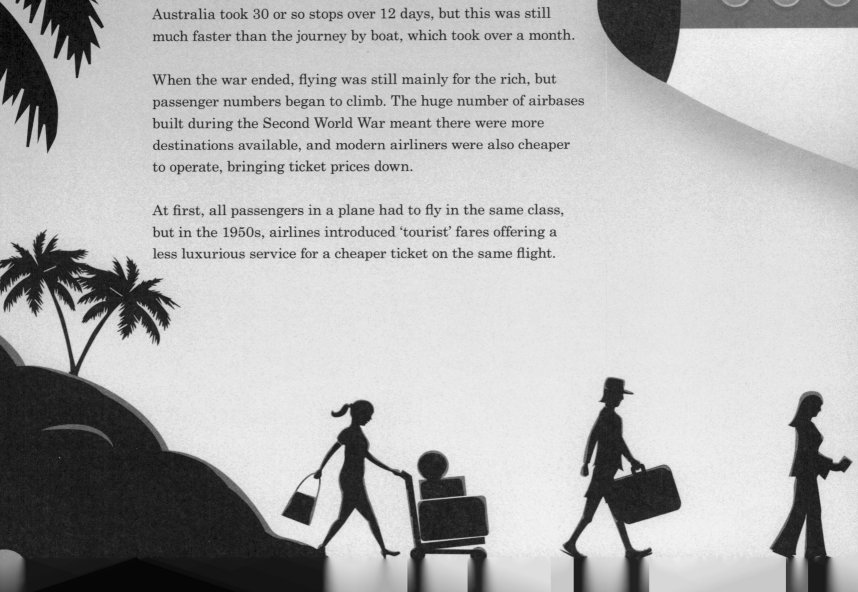

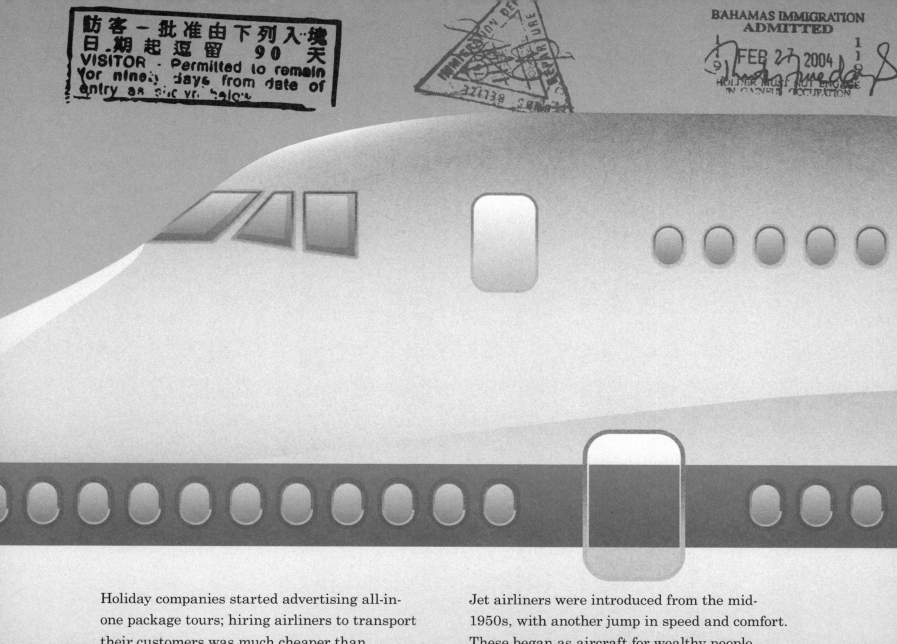

Holiday companies started advertising all-in-one package tours; hiring airliners to transport their customers was much cheaper than booking regular airline flights for all of them. At the same time, rising incomes meant more people could afford to buy tickets.

Jet airliners were introduced from the mid-1950s, with another jump in speed and comfort. These began as aircraft for wealthy people known as 'jet-setters', but when the **BOEING 747** and other wide-body jets arrived in the late 1960s and 1970s, ticket prices tumbled. The era of holiday flights for all was born.

1970

Heroes of the Cabin

THE EARLIEST AIRLINE FLIGHTS HAD NO ONE OTHER THAN THE PILOTS TO LOOK AFTER PASSENGERS, SINCE AEROPLANES ONLY HAD SPACE TO CARRY A FEW PEOPLE.

With passengers often sitting in between mailbags and cargo, flight might have been exciting but it wasn't exactly luxurious. Passenger care had to wait for aircraft with the ability to carry more people.

It wasn't until the 1920s that planes had stewards on board. One of their jobs was to weigh passengers before departure; it was important to know the total weight and balance of the aircraft before take-off!

It was 1930 before women were allowed to join the cabin crew. Ellen Church, a registered nurse with a pilot's licence, convinced the American Boeing Air Transport airline that trained nurses would make ideal flight attendants.

1920s   1930s   1940s   1950s

Though stewardesses were well-paid, it was a tough job. Women were judged on their looks, and could be fired for getting married, gaining weight or simply being 'too old'.

Thankfully, by the 1970s, many of these sexist rules had been outlawed, and married and older flight attendants were allowed to keep their jobs.

Today, cabin crew no longer have to be nurses. But whether evacuating a smoke-filled cabin or dealing with an unruly passenger, stewards are highly trained professionals responsible for the safety of everyone on board.

1960s

1970s

1980s

2000s

A Bag's Journey

AN AIRPORT IS LIKE A BUSY CITY. AIR TRAFFIC CONTROL AND RUNWAYS ARE NEEDED FOR THE AIRCRAFT, WHILE PASSENGERS AND LUGGAGE HAVE TO BE MANAGED TOO.

That means check-in desks, security scanners and baggage handling systems, but also shops, cafés, doctors' stations and prayer rooms. A major airport handles well over 100,000 passengers each day. How does it ensure that each passenger's baggage ends up in the right place?

When a bag is checked in, it receives a label linking it to a passenger and flight. Airline staff put the bag on a conveyor into the baggage handling system. This automatically scans the labels and sends bags on: those checked in early go to a holding facility; those on time go to a sorting station; and bags checked in close to departure are sent directly to the aircraft stand.

There are more than 18 km of conveyor belts to get bags to and from aircraft at London Heathrow's Terminal 5 alone!

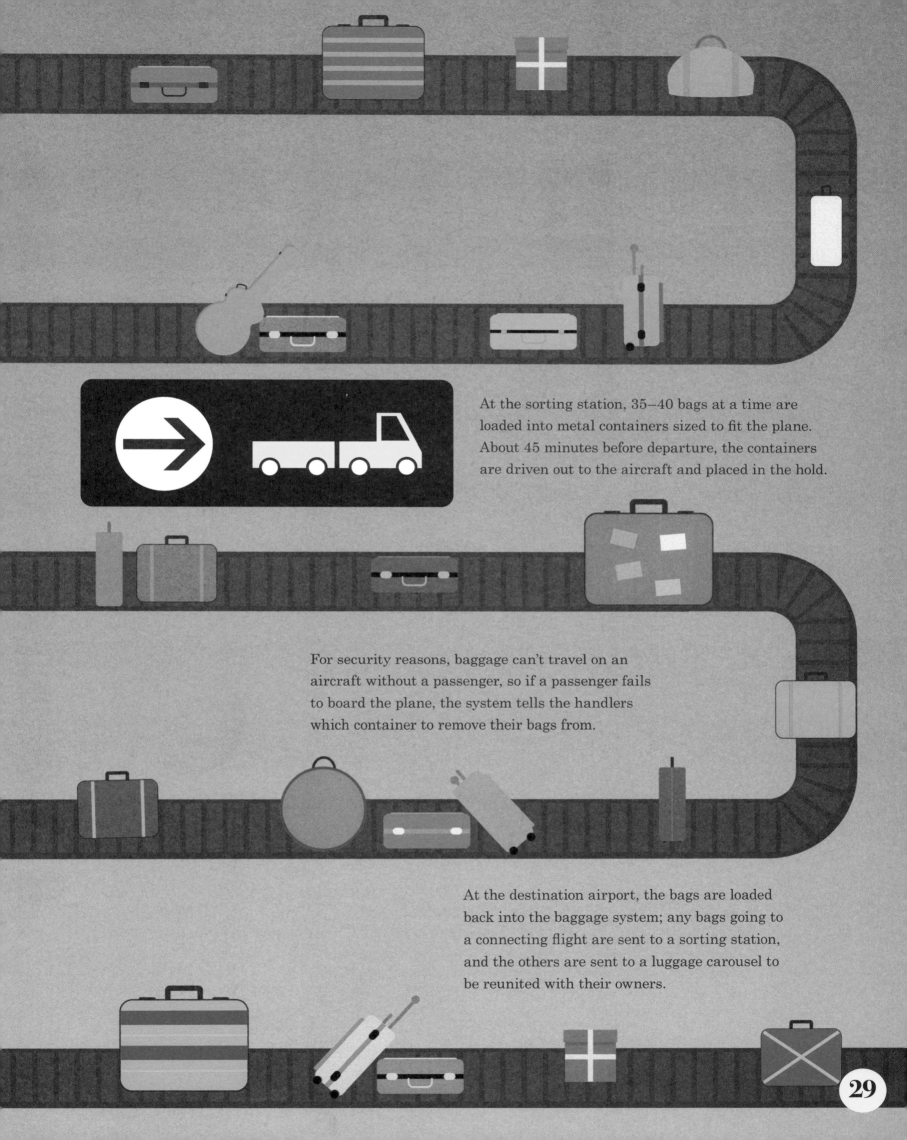

At the sorting station, 35–40 bags at a time are loaded into metal containers sized to fit the plane. About 45 minutes before departure, the containers are driven out to the aircraft and placed in the hold.

For security reasons, baggage can't travel on an aircraft without a passenger, so if a passenger fails to board the plane, the system tells the handlers which container to remove their bags from.

At the destination airport, the bags are loaded back into the baggage system; any bags going to a connecting flight are sent to a sorting station, and the others are sent to a luggage carousel to be reunited with their owners.

Keeping the Skies Safe

THOUGH YOU WON'T FIND ANY LANE MARKINGS OR EXIT SIGNS IN THE AIR, THE PATH AN AEROPLANE TAKES IS STEERED ALONG PARTICULAR ROUTES.

Light aircraft on pleasure flights are allowed to zip across the countryside like buzzing bees, but most passenger air traffic must follow airways at certain speeds and heights for safety's sake.

In the early days of flight, pilots would follow features of the landscape easily visible from the air, such as roads, rivers and railway lines. In the 1920s, the US government built a transcontinental route network for airmail pilots to follow. Towers with illuminated beacons spaced every 5 km allowed pilots to find their way even in the dark. As radio equipment became more widespread, the towers were replaced with a system of radio beacons.

Once a greater number of countries had built radar systems, following the Second World War, it became possible to track the progress of aircraft along invisible 'air corridors'. This ensures that each plane keeps at a safe distance from the next. Air traffic is busiest at airports, so they have their own control areas to keep the flow of aircraft to and from runways smooth. Sometimes the air traffic controllers ask aircraft to circle the airport while they wait to land.

Aircraft only leave the gaze of air traffic controllers on flights across enormous oceans and other sparsely inhabited areas. But even when skies seem clear, the on-board navigation equipment keeps a watchful eye out for other aircraft, and pilots hear the voices of fellow crews crackle across the air waves.

Anatomy of an Aeroplane

THE BASIC LAYOUT OF AN AEROPLANE HAS NOT CHANGED IN NEARLY A CENTURY.

It has wings to keep it in the air; a fuselage for cargo, including passengers and crew; a tail or empennage, for directional stability and control; and an engine or engines for propulsion.

The basic forces on an aircraft are lift, weight, thrust and drag. In steady, level flight, all these forces should balance one another.

LIFT
The force produced by the aircraft's wings, keeping it up in the air.

FUSELAGE

THRUST
Produced by the engine, this force pushes the aircraft forwards.

ENGINE

WEIGHT
The force of gravity pulling the aircraft down.

FLAPS AND SLATS
These extend for take-off and landing, and increase the wing's lift at a given speed, allowing the aeroplane to fly more slowly.

AILERONS
French for 'little wings'. As the pilot moves the controls, these work in opposite directions to make one wing go up and the other down, causing the aircraft to roll.

RUDDER
This moves the tail from side to side and points the aeroplane's nose horizontally.

WING

TAIL

AIRBUS A380

ELEVATORS
These move together to make the tail (and thus the aircraft) go up or down.

DRAG
The force of the air pulling the aircraft backwards.

Building an Aeroplane

MODERN AEROPLANES ARE FEARSOMELY COMPLICATED MACHINES THAT CAN HAVE MILLIONS OF PARTS, AND THEIR DESIGNS ARE OFTEN UPDATED. MANUFACTURING THEM IS A TRICKY BUSINESS.

Setting up machine tools to mass-produce aircraft is expensive and inflexible, so aeroplane builders have always relied on skilled workers to help manufacturing go smoothly. Blueprints and drawings never contain all the information needed to build an aeroplane, so workers use all of their knowledge and experience too.

If lots of aircraft are suddenly needed, as happened during the First and Second World Wars, a shortage in skilled workers can cause problems. In both wars, huge numbers of men and women who had never worked in manufacturing had to be taught how to build aeroplanes.

To avoid a skills shortage problem in the future, and to maintain the right balance between flexibility and speed of production, aeroplane builders became early adopters of manufacturing technologies. These include computer-controlled tools, robotic welders and 3-D printing. However, skilled workers remain at the heart of the production process.

Modern airliners are produced on assembly lines in huge factories. At over 13 million cubic metres, **BOEING'S** Everett Factory in the USA is the largest manufacturing building in the world.

Straight Up

INVENTORS HAD LONG DREAMED OF CREATING AN AIRCRAFT THAT COULD FLY LIKE A HUMMINGBIRD, WHICH CAN HOVER, FLY BACKWARDS OR SIDEWAYS, AND GO UP OR DOWN AT WILL. BUT HOVERING IN THE SAME POSITION IS A CHALLENGE. A HELICOPTER'S ROTOR BLADES SPIN ROUND AND ROUND TO CREATE LIFT.

F-35B LIGHTNING II

5 Jump jets are another way to hover an aircraft: the engine's exhaust nozzles point backwards for forward flight, and swivel downwards to hover and land. As well as swivelling its nozzle, for take-off and landing the *F-35B LIGHTNING II'S* engine powers a fan in the aircraft fuselage for extra lift.

4 Helicopters are slower than fixed-wing aircraft, but transformer-like 'convertiplanes' combine the advantages of both: they take off like helicopters, before tilting their rotors forward to fly like aeroplanes.

AGUSTAWESTLAND AW609

EUROCOPTER EC-145

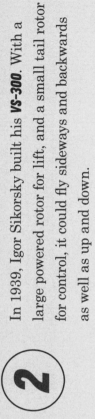

2 In 1939, Igor Sikorsky built his *VS-300*. With a large powered rotor for lift, and a small tail rotor for control, it could fly sideways and backwards as well as up and down.

AUTOGIRO

3 Most modern helicopters use the basic design developed by Sikorsky.

VS-300

1 In 1920, Juan de la Cierva worked out how to steer rotor blades for flight, building his *AUTOGIRO*. The autogiro's unpowered rotor spun like a windmill, so it could only hover in a headwind.

Flying Without Pilots

AUTOPILOTS

Autopilots were first demonstrated in 1914, but it took a while for them to become commercially available. These early systems could fly an aircraft level in one direction, allowing the pilot to briefly concentrate on navigation. In 1933, aviator Wiley Post used an autopilot to become the first person to fly solo around the world, dozing in the cockpit while still keeping on course.

By the late 1940s, development in radar and electronic navigation meant that autopilots could fly programmed courses. In 1947, a US Air Force transport with an experimental autopilot made a transatlantic crossing without the pilot touching the controls!

Modern autopilots can do the same, so they do the bulk of the commercial flying. Today's airliner pilots monitor progress and generally only seize the controls for take-off and landing.

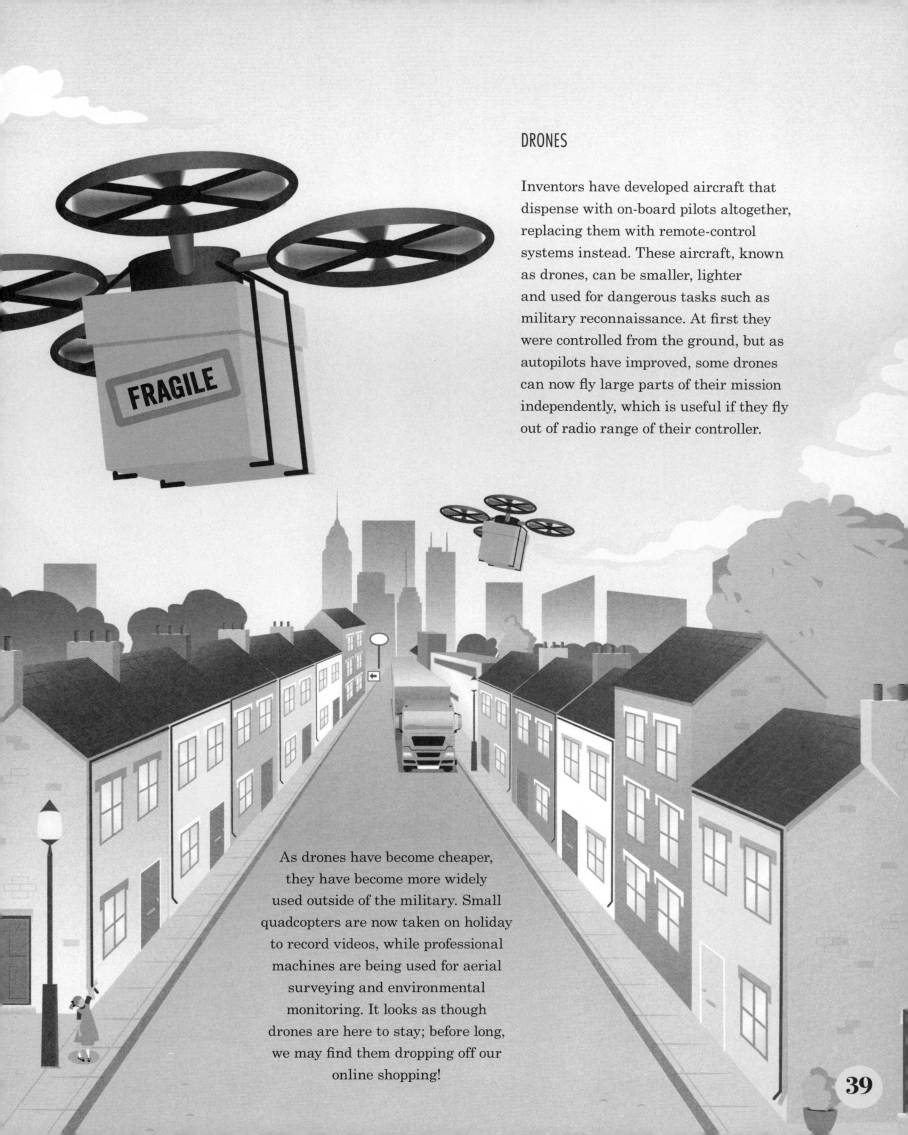

DRONES

Inventors have developed aircraft that dispense with on-board pilots altogether, replacing them with remote-control systems instead. These aircraft, known as drones, can be smaller, lighter and used for dangerous tasks such as military reconnaissance. At first they were controlled from the ground, but as autopilots have improved, some drones can now fly large parts of their mission independently, which is useful if they fly out of radio range of their controller.

As drones have become cheaper, they have become more widely used outside of the military. Small quadcopters are now taken on holiday to record videos, while professional machines are being used for aerial surveying and environmental monitoring. It looks as though drones are here to stay; before long, we may find them dropping off our online shopping!

FRAGILE

Working in the Air

AIRCRAFT ARE USED FOR MANY TASKS BEYOND SIMPLY
TRANSPORTING PASSENGERS AND CARGO.

CROP-DUSTING

Small aircraft are used to spray crops in fields with pesticides
or fertiliser. Fitted with spray equipment and powerful engines,
crop-dusters can pull up sharply at the edges of fields and turn
nimbly to avoid spraying outside the designated area.

AERIAL SURVEYING

From the air, the shape of the land below is revealed in ways
not obvious to those on the ground. Archaeologists can see the
traces of former settlements now buried beneath the earth;
geologists can use specially equipped aircraft to find deposits
of metal ores and other natural resources; and biologists
and ecologists can track migrating animals or see habitats
inaccessible from the ground.

AIR AMBULANCES

In cases where normal ambulances cannot reach the scene quickly enough, specially equipped helicopters carry doctors and paramedics to the scene of an injury, then transport patients to hospital.

EUROCOPTER SUPER PUMA

BERIEV BER 200

FIREFIGHTING

One of the most dramatic roles for an aircraft is that of fighting forest fires. Specialist aircraft are fitted with tanks of water or foam that they can release over a blaze. Some 'flying boats' used for firefighting can skim over the surface of a lake to fill their tanks and take off again without stopping. A converted **BOEING 747** is the world's largest aerial fire-fighter, capable of carrying at least 75 tonnes of water.

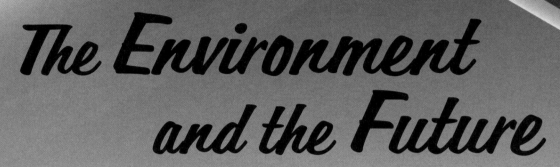

The Environment and the Future

LIKE OTHER FORMS OF TRANSPORT, AIR TRAVEL PRODUCES CARBON DIOXIDE AND OTHER POLLUTANTS SUCH AS NITROUS OXIDES AND PARTICULATES.

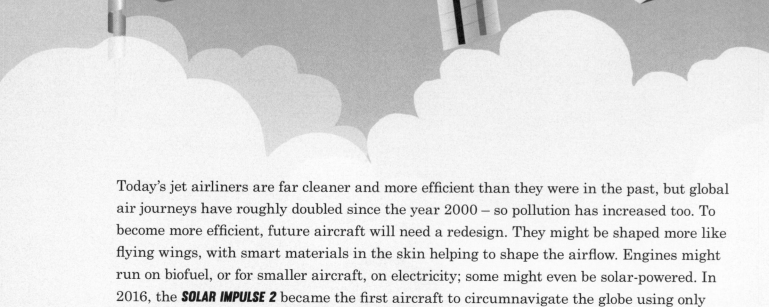

Today's jet airliners are far cleaner and more efficient than they were in the past, but global air journeys have roughly doubled since the year 2000 – so pollution has increased too. To become more efficient, future aircraft will need a redesign. They might be shaped more like flying wings, with smart materials in the skin helping to shape the airflow. Engines might run on biofuel, or for smaller aircraft, on electricity; some might even be solar-powered. In 2016, the **SOLAR IMPULSE 2** became the first aircraft to circumnavigate the globe using only solar power, though it took 17 legs to complete the trip.

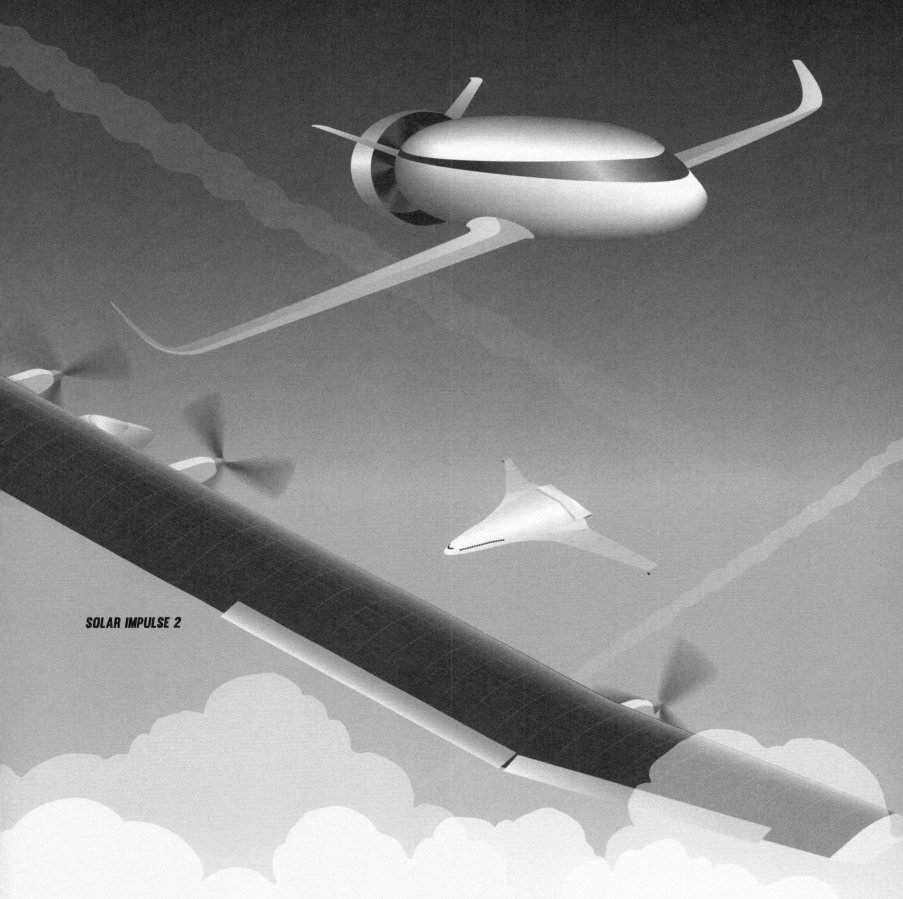

SOLAR IMPULSE 2

New air traffic control systems might allow planes to fly closer together and more efficiently, rather than having to stick to rigid air corridors. Modern airships might take over some cargo routes from aeroplanes – they'd be slower, but better for the environment.

All these technologies will help reduce aviation's environmental impact. As the myths and legends tell us, flight is a precious gift – but one not without its costs. We will have to weigh these as we pursue the dream of flight in the future.

A Short History of the Aeroplane

1910
First successful take-off from on board a ship.

1919
First daily scheduled airline service, from London to Paris.

1925
First in-flight movie shown.

1928
Croydon Airport, in South London, opens the world's first purpose-built airport terminal and control tower.

1939
HEINKEL 176 becomes the first rocket-powered aircraft.

1947

World's first duty-free airport shop opens at Shannon airport in Ireland.

1949

US Air Force **BOEING B-50** makes the first non-stop round-the-world flight.

1956

Production begins on the **CESSNA 172**, the world's most-produced aircraft.

1969

BOEING 747 JUMBO JET first flies, kickstarting the age of mass air travel.

2016

SOLAR IMPULSE 2 completes the first solar-powered round-the-world flight.

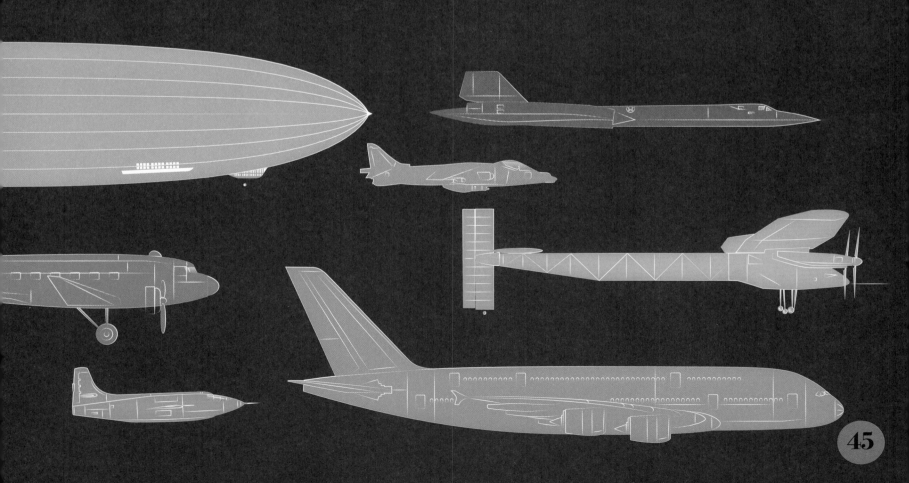

Glossary

ACCELERATE   To go faster; to increase in speed.

AERODYNAMICS   The science of how air moves around objects, and the forces that it creates.

AIR CORRIDOR   An invisible route that airliners fly along, a bit like a motorway in the sky. Usually between two navigation beacons.

ALLOY   Pure metals such as aluminium are usually soft; metal alloys have careful amounts of other elements added to make them stronger. Most aviation alloys are made of aluminium mixed with copper, magnesium, zinc or tin.

AUTOPILOT   A machine that can keep an aeroplane on a steady course without the pilot needing to keep their hands on the controls. More advanced autopilots can fly the aeroplane along complicated paths on their own.

BAGGAGE HANDLING   The work of getting passengers' bags from the airport terminal into an aeroplane.

CARGO   The things that an aeroplane carries, either passenger baggage that is stowed in the hold, or freight containers carried on transport aircraft.

CIRCUMNAVIGATE   To travel all the way around the world.

EFFICIENCY   A measure of how well a machine makes use of the energy that powers it. An efficient aeroplane will use less fuel to travel a given distance and speed than an inefficient one.

GRAVITY   The force that causes objects to fall back down to Earth.

INFRASTRUCTURE   The buildings and systems that support an activity; for air transport these might include airport terminals, runways, radar dishes and radio masts.

JET ENGINE   An engine that uses a jet of hot gases to propel an aircraft.

MANOEUVRABILITY   The ability of an aircraft to change its speed and direction quickly.

NAVIGATION   The skill of working out where you are and which way you need to fly to get to where you want to be. Early navigators used a map and compass; modern aircraft have electronic aids to help them stay on track.

PACKAGE TOUR   A holiday where everything is included in the price, including accommodation and flights to the destination.

POLLUTANT   A substance that harms the environment. Some pollutants are only dangerous in large quantities, or if they get into the wrong place.

PROPULSION   The method of pushing or propelling an aeroplane: propellers, jet engines and rockets are all different kinds of propulsion.

RADAR   A machine that sends out radio waves and detects their reflections, showing the positions of aircraft even in bad weather or at night.

RECONNAISSANCE   Scouting or investigation, to see what is around you or in a particular area.

SOUND BARRIER   As aircraft speeds approach the speed of sound, the drag force on an aeroplane shoots up. When this was first discovered, scientists and engineers described it as a 'sound barrier'. They had to find ways of breaking it before they could fly faster than sound.

Index